Your Guide to be successful in Internet Marketing

Adesesan Odunaya

ISBN: 9781081910662

DEDICATION

I dedicated this book to my family and friends in hustling
ground who are willing to make it big in their online
marketing business

CONTENTS

CONTENTS

your guide to be successful in internet marketing

ACKNOWLEDGMENTS

I give my profound gratitude to God almighty for making this a reality. I also appreciate my mum and dad who has been my light in this world. without them this might not be possible.

CHAPTER ONE

Insight on Internet Marketing

Today's world requires us to embrace the reality that every business competes for a customer's attention. This is where marketing enters the picture to play a crucial role in increasing a clientele's size and interest. Domestic and international markets have become oversaturated with suppliers, producers, and intermediaries as a result of the progressive rise in the number of small and major firms that have emerged over the past 20 years. These businesses are all competing to be the first to reach the chain's finish.

The idea of marketing was heavily attacked up until a few years ago. Many saw it as nothing more than a waste of money that could have been invested instead of wasted. in producing and developing a sales force. Instead of creating a pull that customers could not resist, this sales-oriented strategy forces enterprises to push goods and services onto the market.

Marketing is able to accomplish that. Promoting products and services through cleverly conceived strategies and concepts gradually started to play a significant part in a company's overall purpose, reaching sales goals and raising much-needed awareness. As a result, the function of physical marketing was better understood. Without a genuine marketing strategy in place, a successful business cannot even consider creating goods and services today.

Marketing is therefore a company's arsenal against a market consisting of picky, exacting, and inquisitive consumers. It aids the company in providing information, addressing issues, outlining solutions, and fostering enduring relationships with clients. Online marketing is a concept that has emerged in the twenty-first century that is similar.

The saturation of the market discussed here has led to the transition to a virtual environment. As more companies sought to draw clients, the internet emerged as a successful platform for reaching a wide audience.and to promote a single good or service through various platforms and viewpoints. Online marketing quickly developed into a sizable sector that now generates billions of dollars in revenue from advertising.

However, embracing online marketing as a standard practice has not been simple for many traditional firms, just as many struggled to appreciate the significance and necessity of physical marketing methods.and to spread awareness of a single commodity or service through a variety of media and points of view. Online marketing swiftly grew to be a significant industry that currently brings in billions of dollars every year through advertising.

For many traditional businesses, adopting online marketing as a routine practice hasn't been easy, just as many found it difficult to see the value and importance of old methods of physical marketing.marketing Methods of physical marketing are still unclear to the public. While the early adopters of internet marketing, as well as millions of firms globally, have hopped on board, one million more are still debating whether it is worthwhile to do so.

This e-book will demonstrate how helpful it is to learn what web marketing actually is and how this cutting-edge tactic might raise a company from being merely average to amazing.1

What exactly is online marketing?wOnline marketing, sometimes known as internet marketing, is the process of promoting products and services online. The internet serves as a channel for communication.

However, just like many struggling to understand the importance and need for physical marketing strategies, adopting online marketing as a norm has not been easy for many oldschool businesses. Since they have been functioning just fine with a brick and mortar presence, for them, online marketing might seem quite unnecessary. How can this perception be changed? What is it that marketers can do to create and increase awareness about online marketing? The answer is quite simple. Ask an average individual about online marketing; they may stop for a second or two to collect their thoughts before giving an answer. The concept of online marketing is not quite clear to people yet. While millions of businesses worldwide have jumped on the bandwagon of online marketing, not to mention the early adopters of this practice, a million others are still contemplating whether it is worth adopting. This e-book will prove how useful understanding what online marketing actually is, and it will look at how this modern technique can help to spring a business up from being average to extraordinary.

CHAPTER TWO

What is internet marketing?

Internet marketing, or online marketing, refers to the promotion of goods and services on the internet. The online world acts as a medium to communicate Executive Summary messages that a business drafts for its audience. Online marketing is also synonymous with online advertising. It is essential to understand that online marketing is not second to traditional marketing. Nor is it a complimentary service that you can use to boost your If you are not happy with your current ERP software, you are likely researching and marketing efforts on other mediums. Instead, online marketing is a hardcore way to promote a business and make it known to an audience that is bombarded with tons of similar stimuli every minute of the day. evaluating other ERP options. Because each manufacturer has specific business challenges, Perhaps the very foundation of online marketing lies in finding newer ways to reach customers and markets that would be interested in what a business has to each has a different path when finding the perfect ERP solution. Below are seven reasons offer. Since traditional mediums like newspaper, prints and TVs have been tried over and over again, a new and creative internet marketing idea seems to be the fresh start that modern businesses so desperately need. My patched together QuickBooks and Excel spreadsheets are Another reason why internet marketing has gained so much momentum in the last few years is that, by using this method, many companies and business preventing my business from growing. owners aim to break the clutter that has piled up because of nonstop marketing efforts. Every company and every business, in an attempt to attract customers, indulge in various marketing tactics, like an ad in the local newspaper or a TVs campaign that can be viewed on various channels. When combined, all these campaigns lead to an overload and customers usually become resistant to such attempts. Internet marketing provides a different My homegrown/custom system has become unmanageable, lacks way to do the same activities, and cash in on high consumer interest as well. Coupled with this, increased internet usage is another factor that has made this marketing alternative quite a hit. modern features and customization has made upgrades impossible. According to statistics, 80% of the people in the United States use the internet regularly. Out of these, 97% use it to search for products that they eventually end up buying. Google research reveals that 10.3 billion searches are conducted online result in nine out of 10 product/business follow-ups. With such high rates of internet usage and the possibility of customers getting back to you, wouldn't you want your small business to have a face in the realm of the World Wide Web? owner is discontinuing the system and ending development and support. However, the dilemma comes in when owners of small business, who rightly play the part of marketer, administrator and finance office as well, voice that they do not have time to keep their online presence updated. With such a bleak outlook of even trying to take advantage of the internet, these companies often ignore one of the biggest consumer touch points of the 21st century. tools and compliance programs, such as lot tracking and quality control. Not only does such a business let go of an opportunity to grow and mature with the market, it also sets itself up to lose to the competition. Businesses that compete with you, directly or indirectly, can make tremendous profits and convert potential sales leads into loyal customers by taking advantage of being present on the internet. My ERP software is not manufacturing-specific and lacks the features and modules my shop floor needs. Therefore, it is essential for a small business working in the global economy to make use of internet marketing. Even if you do not have the resources to spend on an e-commerce website, at least make sure you are listed in the online yellow pages directory. When customers conduct a quick search for the product they want, your company name will be displayed.

My ERP solution lacks the planning and scheduling functionality to Approximately 48% of all customers using the internet to search for businesses use the Yellow Pages Directory, which is available online. As it will be dramatically increase capacity without adding floor space, employees many ways to market your business on the internet, using either free or paid solutions depending on the budget you have to assign to internet marketing. Using these methods is an excellent way to make sure you are heard and seen on the internet. My technology is old, my hardware is unreliable and we are experiencing Online marketing has become a mandatory part of a business's promotional strategy. No campaign is complete without a representation on the internet. Leaving out this medium means giving up your customers to the competitor!

Being a primary source of information for millions of people, the internet opens up avenues to look for products and businesses by breaking geographic boundaries. No longer does a user have to be physically present in a locality to make use of the products sold by a local business. Tapping into newer markets is one of the biggest advantages of internet marketing.

Therefore, making sure that an online promotional campaign is thorough and appealing is essential. Sending across the same message via various techniques and channels on the internet is a must. There are many types of online marketing that have evolved and developed over the years, keeping in mind the way this medium is used by consumers.

For instance, when the internet was a basic tool that was used by only a handful of people with access to it, online marketing was one-dimensional, meaning, one long advertisement about a product would be put up on a single website or search engine for visitors to see. As usage increased, so did the complexity associated with the internet marketing.

Today, a single advert hardly suffices for the many sub-mediums that have sprung up on the internet. Social media, websites, search engines, yellow pages, and website directories are some of the many channels on which a business needs to advertise in a creative manner, keeping in mind the kind of audience that visits them.

Hence, online marketing consists out of the following subtypes of online marketing:

CHAPTER THREE

Email marketing

This refers to marketing that is done by sending advertisements and promotional content through emails. Businesses usually maintain email directories for email marketing.

Search Engine Optimization (SEO)

This refers to increasing the visibility of a website, its content or the words within the content so that they appear in search results. This is done using on-page and off-page optimization. Search Engine Marketing (SEM) This refers to the increasing website's visibility in the search engines using paid reach (paid advertising) and organic reach (SEO) his refers to promoting a business on social media, such as Facebook, LinkedIn and Twitter.

Affiliate Marketing

It refers to the hiring of third parties, also called affiliates, who market a business's content online. 18 The details of these types of marketing will be discussed thoroughly in separate chapters of this book.

Online marketing trends

One of the biggest advantages of online marketing is the flexibility it offers to businesses. Unlike the high cost and complex process typical for traditional marketing efforts, internet marketing can be cheaper and easily accessible to most web owners, who are skilled enough to take advantage of different.

1. Why Should You Leave QuickBooks and Invest In Your First ERP Software?

techniques of online marketing. While TVs and outdoor campaigns are somewhat standardized, online promotion strategies can be adjusted according to customers' reactions and responses.

Depending on what generates the best results, online advertising follows certain patterns. While these patterns may remain the same for an indefinite period Leaving behind the familiarity of QuickBooks and Excel spreadsheets might seem like of time, usually they change and fluctuate based on how the market for particular goods and services is performing and on the way consumers behave in taking off the training wheels for your business. Though this solution has worked well in general. For instance, if customers buying online diet packages are satisfied with their purchases that they made after watching videos, the trend for visuals the past, there comes a time in every manufacturer's life that scheduling whiteboards and therefore, just like any other business, online marketing also experiences shifts in what is needed and what should be antiquated. Some of the most popular online marketing trends at this point, that have been highlighted by experts, based on the current developments in the online world, are the following: The QuickBooks path is common for young businesses. It begins with Excel spreadsheet and a manual whiteboard, and as the company grows and matures, a reliable accounting One of the most prominent shifts in online marketing has been from desktops and laptops to mobile devices. No longer do people sit in front of computers all package such as QuickBooks is integrated into the mix. day long to search for products or read reviews about a business. In fact, the year 2016 brought a new milestone - the number of mobile users has finally surpassed the number of desktop users. Successful online businesses have foreseen this trend and have launched websites that are compatible for mobile phones. Similarly, customizing content for smartphones and tablets is also a new trend that has been initiated by the popularity and preference for integrated devices.

Unfortunately, there is a limit to how far QuickBooks can take you. Eventually, you need to make purchases in the last few years. Whatever content it may be, if it is available for your customers to view and enjoy on the go, it will be enough to sustain their new business management solution that can support the growth of your business, which interests you. If, on the other hand, your small business is not onboard for this change, it is likely to lose key customers and markets. Additionally, Google now takes "mobile-friendliness as a ranking signal on mobile searches", which is yet another reason why mobile friendly websites are a must in the online market nowadays.is why you should invest in Enterprise Resource Planning (ERP) software. An ERP software Less is more system increases visibility throughout the whole company, allowing for quicker decisions Gone are the days when the quantity of advertisements and promotions signified strength and a solid market standing. The same applies to in-depth and making and more opportunities to grow the business.

Comprehensive advertisement campaigns that would just go on and on! Simplicity is the key to making online marketing work for your brand. Customers are now looking for quick and short ads that are attractive and alluring at the same time.

Look at some of the most famous everyday brands that advertise online. Do they have neverending campaigns that bore you so much that you feel like Comprehensive ERP software serves as single data storage for all aspects of your business skipping the promotional message altogether? by integrating CRM, financials and production all in one place. With automated workflow Brands like Apple and Google create simple, straightforward ads. However, they are designed creatively, with an allure that catches customer attention. The tools, you don't have to wait for other departments to bring you batched information to "more is less" slogan also works so well because customers are already overwhelmed with a lot of promotional information day in and day out. If your message stands out with simplicity and creativity, it will get the most attention. upload. Your ERP software can automatically update inventory levels, sales orders, capacity

CHAPTER FOUR

Integrated imaging and content publication

A combination of content and images is an important shift from content-only online advertising. Placing emphasis on certain points within the content is Unlike QuickBooks, ERP software is fully scalable and will grow with your business, rather intelligently done by breaking it up with images. Image marketing has always been a useful way to attract attention from customers who do not like to read, rather than limit the number of users you are allowed. QuickBooks has been known to have a lot of content. Using this strategy in a creative manner will definitely optimize the promotional campaigns for success. In general, websites that have a blog functionality issues as more concurrent users sign in to the system. and publish content regularly receive more links, traffic and leads, which all together adds up to better performance.

Evolution of video format

During the past couple of years, video as a format of content reached its peak, shifting the focus of online marketers again. Development of technology and ERP software is designed to keep your shop floor running at the most optimal levels. The need for visualization, together with the evolution of social media platforms, and their live video feature enabled this trend to become the dominant trend in online marketing. Summary Example, powerful ERP software can automatically load your schedule, taking into account material constraints, BOM complexity, WIP processes, tooling conflicts and priority orders, Online marketing is a necessity. In a world where e-commerce has become the single biggest reason for businesses to build an online presence, the need to market products and services online is paramount. However, it should be remembered at all times that the internet is a product of modernization and change. while simultaneously evaluating the resources required to meet demand and allow for For this reason, it does not take long for new trends and shifts to materialize.

Being a business that markets online, you have to make sure that you innovate constantly, without letting your online presence become outdated. Since

millions of businesses have made the move to the virtual world, internet marketing has started to become cluttered, just like traditional marketing.

Therefore, if ERP software can eliminate unnecessary teardowns and resets while optimizing production What businesses need to master to make sure their online marketing efforts reap results include: Creativity Out of the box ideas runs. With the ERP software's RealTime™ automatic production monitoring module collecting data at each work center, you can catch and respond to defect issues before they require costly re-runs. Constant planning High degree of flexibility Keeping up with the current trends Constant research and analysis In the same breath, also keep in mind that using the many channels of online marketing is not an option. In fact, cashing in on the different dynamics, An ERP system's business activity monitoring capabilities can notify you if you begin working, and characteristics of each are essential to make sure you build an impressive reputation for the business and loyalty amongst the customers. Lastly, being educated about the latest trends of online marketing keeps a business up-to-date with how its market thinks, reacts and responds to various running out of a particular inventory item or if one of your production lines fails. It can also campaign. Online marketing departs from traditional marketing in that the former is geared towards not only creating hype, but also being available whenever introduce business intelligence capabilities to your business' day-to-day operations, with

forecasting tools, Statistical Process Control (SPC) analysis and dashboards tailored to 22 your needs.

CHAPTER FIVE

Web Analytics

Introduction

The proliferation of internet usage and the upsurge in the creation of so many websites has led to the development of an entire science devoted to the understanding of the patterns online. Most users are comfortable with the idea of interacting with a non-human structure, the website, which is giving them access to information and allowing them to conduct different operations.

The website is like a portal that opens up a range of possibilities for the users. There are a lot of different kinds of static and dynamic websites, which allow varying ranges of interaction and entertainment. Usually people do not realize that at the backend of their internet usage and browsing is being recorded in If you manufacture for an industry that is heavily regulated and requires you to meet certain different statistical forms so that the website owner could know more about the visitors on the website. quality standards, an ERP system can greatly assist in that area, too. With lot and serial This systematic approach to finding out more about users of your website is broadly known as web analytics. Through web analytics there is an attempt to gauge how the website content affects the users and how the users respond to different types of stimuli on the web page. Monitoring the users' activity and the traceability, audit tools, electronic signatures and document control, ERP software systems site's performance are some of the most important functions of web analytics. In order to find out about the online activity of the users, their preferences and are invaluable for auditing and achieving high-level compliance. their tastes, web analytic tools are extensively used. Market research is another area where this data is extremely relevant. What is web analytics? ERP packages come in various levels of sophistication and price. There is a next step Web analytics basically refers to the usage of web data for analysis and understanding of online patterns. For web analytics, the data is collected, measured and then interpreted. Web traffic is gauged and measured by using different types of instruments. The number of people who visit a website and the type of out there for every QuickBooks user, but you are cautioned against taking too small of an activity they conduct while using that website is recorded consistently so that the website developers can analyze which aspects are interesting and which ones need to be modified. Web analytics is used to assess the effectiveness of the content placed online.

Employee training and business practice effectiveness. Choose a package and a provider that can grow with your business.

An area where this study of web traffic is gaining widespread popularity is that of e-commerce. Businesses use this information as an easy and cost effective

way to conduct large-scale market research without directly bothering their existing or potential customers. Advertising is another area where this data Moving away from QuickBooks and into an ERP software system will give you the confidence becomes extremely relevant because a business can assess and measure user response directly after the introduction of a new ad or offer. The data also provides gainful information about the demographics of the users and this information can be used to inform the operational decisions of the firm. in your data. You can now rely on one system that doesn't involve third party vendors or Such type of research has implications for what the business produces, what it sells, how it sells and to whom it sells. Broadly, the types of metrics measured limited scalability. Choose an ERP provider that provides a holistic view of your operations. by web analytic instruments include the number of people who visit a website, number of pages viewed, number of clicks, etc.

Off-site web analytics

This type of collection and assessment of data measures the general online performance of a website regardless of whether one owns or maintains it. The popularity and the attention the website gathers on the internet outside the sphere of the website's own operations is measured by off-site web analytics. This information provides a guideline regarding the status of the website on the internet, its audience, visibility and buzz.

On-site web analytics

This type of data strictly deals with the information that is collected when users visit a site and how they interact with different elements present on the web pages. The duration of their stay and the translation of their interest into purchases or subscription can also be measured. One can also find out about the landing pages, which entice the buyer into making a purchase. Onsite web analytics are particularly important for commercial purposes where businesses want to know exactly the worth of their investment. The most widely used tool for measuring on-site response of users is Google Analytics. Two methods are used for managing on-site analytics. Firstly, the log file method was used in which the server records the requests of the visitors in a log file and then these can be read. Another method known as page tagging is used more often at present. In page tagging, when a page loads and when something is clicked on the website, this is registered in the web analytics by embedding JavaScript in the code.

Reasons for using web analytics

Websites that deal with the provision of a lot of content, textual or otherwise, did not have a clear-cut means of finding or knowing how much the discourse available on their website was worth. In business terms, measuring the return on investment of content has been made possible by using sophisticated web analytics. In order to gauge the worth of your website content, qualitative and quantitative analysis are both important.

Quantitative and qualitative analysis

Quantitative analysis gives information regarding the numerical and statistical value of the content by telling the business what the users do, while qualitative analysis will help the business see how the users engage with the content. It can tell you about the purpose of the user's visit and the effectiveness of your content. Web analytics allow website content developers to get great insights into what to present to the users in order to increase their web traffic.

Content planning

Web analytics can be used in the realm of content planning in order to find out which type of items or elements might be problematic or redundant. Using this data, it becomes easy to compare and review one's own performance with the performance of a past period. It becomes easy to use these numbers in order to sketch out a trend of growth for your business. If the website is not getting enough traffic and your business is considering a serious remodeling, web analytics can help you understand whether this might be a viable investment or not.

Websites can also find out whether their users are satisfied or not.

Those who create the content will obviously be interested in knowing how successful it is because they can use this knowledge to make decisions about the future content they produce. Influence on marketing decisions

Marketing is an important area that is affected by the results of web analysis. Website owners can clearly find out how users are reaching their website, i.e. through another website or a different link. This way, they can use these channels to market their products and services.

For instance, if a clothes retailer gets most of its users redirected from its Facebook page, then it is safe to assume that marketing on the Facebook page should be more rigorous.

In order to calculate whether an advertising campaign was successful or not, websites can make good use of insightful data from web analytics. Websites usually function as international portals of information and they can discover the geographical location of their visitors by analyzing data. This way their strategies and content can be modified to suit the cultural, ethical or personal characteristics of the users it attracts.

Various subtopics of web analytics: methods of measuring

web traffic

However, It is imperative for website owners to gauge the performance of their website based on the metrics displayed in the table above. Knowing the visitor type is significant because there are some people who visit your site for the first time while others are regular. Calculating unique visitors and unique sessions is equally important for the website. The unique visitors were calculated by using cookies and this helped analysts to trace individual consumer behavior. equally important for the website. The unique visitors were calculated by using cookies and this helped analysts to trace individual consumer behavior. However, the second approach in which unique sessions are calculated is more suitable for commercial needs because in each new session a business can market its product or service to the users, whether those are new or a regular visitors. There are eight common metrics for website analysis and these are displayed in the table below:

Average Time On Site (ATOS)

The average time spent on a website is another technique to gauge how long users are really browsing the material. Users who stay for less than 5 seconds and those who spend more than 5 minutes are among the metrics that are used.

Why Every Company Eventually Outgrows its Own-Born Software System: Internal Search 2

Websites also use internal searches to learn more about their visitors. You can search for the material by putting your query into the internal search box, which is essentially a feature provided to users to allow for site-specific searches. Websites can utilize this information to determine what goods and services to offer, which goods should be made more easily available, what the majority of customers prefer, what problems they encounter, etc. The platform is able to provide individualized offers and even use It is simple to comprehend how locally developed ERP software systems started.

Businesses reviewed were seeking. These businesses decided to construct a Here is another important tool for knowing how customers approach your website and what they do once they get there instead of paying more than they felt comfortable with or changing their Visitor path business processes to fit the program. It is crucial for e-commerce companies to develop their own system using internal staff, allies, or regional programmers.

to be aware of any issues that may arise along the process of a user choosing an item, adding it to their basket, and making a transaction. Understanding that the users' actions are not always logical and can occasionally be random is another way to approach this.

Tracing the visitor's path back to the source is the only way to comprehend the

These businesses were encouraged by their early success and later merged their software with the last page the user had been browsing. People today typically read several articles or items on various websites before clicking on anything. They had access to the source code of this accounting program. Another indicator is the number of years that have passed and the top pages, which include the top pages for site entry, exit, and popularity. It is simple to comprehend why base intuitively.

Within a short period of time, the business had three programmers and a few local consultants. Optimizing content for top entry pages and popular pages is crucial, and top exit pages enable content developers to detect and remove system workings. issues that users are having. The analysts can also match the top pages on a website with the business objectives; for example, if the top pages are the secondary pages and don't actually help boost sales, the business's objectives aren't being met. But then crucial components start to fall apart. Referrers, which assist a user in finding a website, are among the other crucial metrics that the accounting package may run out of. But then crucial components start to fall apart. Referrers, which assist a user in finding a website, are among the other crucial metrics that the accounting package may run out of. This can be done through social media platforms, personal bookmarks, search engine results, links on other websites, links on blogs, etc. Consider the positioning of the date and is no longer compliant if the referrer is not generating enough traffic. The operating system or coding tools might no longer be available. it's link. The use of keywords is yet another crucial technique that aids content creators in learning about the most popular words and phrases, which they can subsequently support with vendor assistance. In order to increase traffic, a key programming employee or consultant retires, eliminating their ability to include in their own content. Finally, pinpointing mistakes is crucial to fixing any issues or weaknesses on your website since if users consistently see difficulties when the page loads, they may stop using it. their innate knowledge. The business that uses log files is at danger because the indigenous system may turn out to be an expensive undertaking.

The first sort of web analysis, known as log-file analysis, was based on counting the number of hits a webpage had. In the middle of the 1990s, requests from a single user every 30 minutes were known as page views, requests to view a page, and visits/sessions. The same is true of customized systems. A business purchases a capable ERP package from a local vendor after haggling and successfully obtaining the rights to the source code, allowing them to customize idleness, were also employed as measuring tools. On websites, web counters that displayed how frequently a site had been visited were also widely utilized. The system is becoming increasingly more customized to their preferences. Over time, the merchant can cease to operate your system.

Using Internet Protocol Intelligence, the location, city, and postal code of the visitor are determined. The type of connection, the identity of the Internet service provider, and proxy information can all be ascertained using this technique. Market segmentation and behavioral targeting for firms have become easy thanks to the use of this data. Local businesses can benefit greatly from geolocation analysis as it may direct website visitors to their actual location.

This group includes tracking website users' click patterns. The websites of today go beyond simple HTML pages. They consist of a variety of groups of pages with different levels of interactivity, such as photo, video, and connection galleries. Owners of websites are enthusiastic about galleries, videos, multiple links and several sets of pages with varying levels of interactive elements. Website owners are interested in knowing what users commonly click on, so they can then probe into the reasons behind greater attention being given to some elements over the other. Things like placement of objects, sequences, navigation, text style and visibility, color and design can all be assessed by these metrics. If more users tend to click on something, it is obviously representative of their interest in that item.

The click analytics process can happen in real time where editors tailor the content of the website immediately to garner more clicks. This can happen if there is a discount or sales offer on a website and editors manage the content in real time to attract as many customers as possible. Click analysis can also be done in unreal time, which gives a general picture of the performance of different elements on the website. Clicks are collected at the backend by logging the click when it happens or by considering that every page view is the result of a click.

.

CHAPTER SIX

Google Analytics

One of the most popular tools used by different websites and businesses for analyzing the web traffic is Google Analytics, a free service, using which websites can get insights about their users. One can find out about their traffic sources, conversation rate, etc. The return on advertisement, performance of referrers among many of the old system's pain points was the absence of a strong electronic Data and success of email marketing can also be seen. It provides in-depth reports and motion charts for about 50 sites per user profile. Commerce related metrics such as revenue and sales are also presented. In addition, it provides tools for search engine optimization (SEO). Interchange (EDI) program required by Mar-Bal's customers. Inventory control with the old system was also sorely deficient. The inability to scan inventory from the shop floor included redundant data entry and unavoidable data entry errors. To round it all out, the old In essence, web analytics is about collating and interpreting website traffic, which is receiving widespread attention from different circles. As more websites' ERP systems contain very limited reporting tools and forecasting abilities with no way to spring up, people want to know the return on their investment and they want to tailor their content to gather more online attention, which would obviously easily segregate the separate plants' costs and sales.

Marketing, advertising and e-commerce are some of the areas where the reports from web analysts are used. Web analytics is of two types, off-site and on-site. There are four basic metric categories known as site usage, referrers, site content analysis and quality assurance. Mar-Bal had two options: pour more money into its outdated system and attempt to evaluate and record the performance of a website in order to create a comprehensive report focused on some of the following goals: manually streamline processes in its manufacturing system or find a new ERP provider. Efficiency of website content Site usability Learning about the target audience Quality traffic Referrals Conversion rate Social reports E-commerce reportingMar-Bal chose the latter and the search began for a modern system with more capabilities that wouldn't add more operational costs to the existing organization. Mar-Bal selected a manufacturing-specific ERP and MES solution from an established ERP vendor.

After implementation, Mar-Bal's total annual savings were $270,000 across its four plants The Basics of Conversion Optimization As well as nearly 5,000 potential machine hours that were no longer lost to downtime for monthly physical inventory audits.

The Basics of Conversion Optimization Like most manufacturers, Mar-Bal, Inc. was ready to significantly grow its business. The Introduction company realized that its homegrown, customized system was holding it back; therefore, The concept of conversion optimization is very valuable to online marketers. To understand what this term means, let us first discuss the importance of online. They took the steps necessary to find and implement a new, modern ERP solution.

touchpoints. A touchpoint, in business terms, is a medium where the customer first engages with a business, gets to know about it or explores its product offering. The importance of a touchpoint is paramount because it gives the audience a first impression about a business – how well it receives, engages and attracts them to take action. One of the most primary consumer touchpoints is a business's website. Every online business first develops a website that gives information about the business to those who are interested. A fully functional business website is an interactive channel that lets customers explore the business and get in touch with it.

Therefore, a website is the face of a business in the virtual world and the better it looks, the more it attracts. Conversion optimization or conversion rate optimization (CRO) has to do with corporate websites. How well these websites are geared to attract customers is what CRO determines in a very unique manner. What is CRO and how does it work? These details will be discussed next. However, do remember that CRO is a well-balanced qualitative and quantitative assessment that is used by expert online marketers to make sure their promotional efforts yield positive results.

CHAPTER SEVEN

What is conversion optimization?

Conversion optimization is a process particularly used by websites, forums and landing pages. To define this term fully, let us break it down. Firstly, conversion is the specific action you want your web visitors/browsers to take. What kind of action could this be?

Action refers to what you ideally want your customers to do when they visit your website. It may be: Calling your customer service department Clicking on 'purchase' Downloading the displayed program Registering for a newsletter Referring a friend Registering with an email and password

Next, conversion rate optimization refers to the rate at which visitors, browsing your website, convert to customers.

In other words, CRO aims to bring about required action as a result of passive web browsing. Therefore, CRO is a systematic method to improve the performance of your website to increase the rate at which action is taken.

Website performance is an accumulation of many factors, called key performance indicators. These indicators are responsible for attracting traffic to the webpage and interesting visitors enough so that they browse through. CRO can be applied to all or any one KPI that is determined to be underperforming. From the customer's point of view, CRO is used to figure out what users and customer want to see on the webpage, what entices them to take action and what they believe is lacking on it. The carefully calculated and analyzed results of CRO are then implemented to make these changes. CRO is a structured approach that takes into account a number of things to achieve desired results. The majority of the findings derived in the conversion rate optimization process come from: Consumer and expert insights User feedback An impartial analysis of the website by a professional Web analytics tools 36 Using information from these sources, CRO brings about required changes by keeping in mind the objectives you have set for the website. For instance, if all you want users to do is create an account,

CRO will aim to increase the chances of it happening, instead of introducing a completely new objective. Conversion rate optimization is then a strategy, a plan of action that changes the perceptions of the audience about a website by giving it what it needs to take action. In this light, CRO is a very comprehensive approach that includes even the smallest alterations made to a webpage. It can be either the positioning of the call-to-action button or completing restructuring the steps of a recruitment process. CRO comes in play when a business feels that something is stopping potential sales leads from converting. Such a situation arises when you record heavy traffic flow on your forum, but only a handful take an action. Moreover, behavior patterns of consumer groups vary widely from one channel to the other. Online marketing response rates fluctuate one hour to the next and most of the times, from one offer to the other. 6

Very aptly put, CRO is a combination of art and science. The science comes from knowing which changes to initiate, which KPIs to measure and how to run tests to see the effect of a particular change. On the other hand, the art comes from making the website aesthetically appealing to visitors, designing attractive call-to-action buttons and the best feedback routes to engage customers. marketing response rates fluctuate one hour to the next and most of the times, from one offer to the other. Very aptly put, CRO is a combination of art and science. The science comes from knowing which changes to initiate, which KPIs to measure and how to run 6 tests to see the effect of a particular change. On the other hand, the art comes from making the website aesthetically appealing to visitors, designing attractive call-to-action buttons and the best feedback routes to engage customers.

CHAPTER EIGHT

What conversion optimization is not

There are many things that do not define CRO, but are wrongly affixed with its definition and understanding. As mentioned previously, CRO is an analytical process that takes into account solid feedback and important details of KPIs of the website and the business.

Therefore, CRO is not about: Guesses, hopes and hunches What others might be doing What the CEO thinks about the website Increasing the number of visitors without paying attention to quality of

Legacy ERP Systems: The Backstory Some important terms to remember, since conversion optimization is a combination of science and art, there are many jargons related to this online marketing assessment methodology that need to be understood to make sense of CRO. Most of these terms are a repeated occurrence in CRO related discussions because without them, the process of A legacy ERP system is an older enterprise software that is largely no longer being enhanced. Legacy ERP systems were usually first created in the 1980s or early 1990s and were often based on older technology, such as PIC, Progress or DOS. Their original user interfaces If you were familiar with how websites are created, you would know what CTA buttons are. As the name suggests, call-to-action buttons are the highlighted buttons or links on a webpage that let you perform an action. For instance, a 'Buy Now' button on an e-commerce website that converts you from a surfer to a were character-based, though many received facelifts over the years, often using Windows. Customers fall under this category. CTA buttons are of all shapes, colors and sizes, depending on what the need is, and depending on the nature of the market clients to provide some degree of modern UI look and feel. Most also have some sort of website targeted towards them. Some popular examples are 'Register Now' buttons, 'Sign Up' buttons, 'Book Now' buttons and 'Download Now' buttons. bolt-on business intelligence tool for improved reporting and analytics. Conversion funnel The conversion flow is the path taken by visitors from when they visit your website until the action is taken, i.e. conversion takes place. For an e-commerce Legacy ERP systems typically have rich, industry-specific business functionality. Their website the conversion funnel will be the following path: homepage - search product - product page – checkout - payment. Knowing the conversion funnel for creators continued writing application code to meet the needs of existing customers. an action is very important because all changes and improvements are then made to the various elements of the funnel during the CRO process. 38 However, they did not reformat the system to modern technology, eventually making the system outdated. A/B Tests In the years between 2000 and 2010, it was commonplace for legacy system founders A/B testing is a statistical approach to CRO that takes into account two variables at one point in time. The effectiveness of both, A and B, is then gauged when to sell their businesses to larger software companies. It was a sound exit strategy for the customers to respond to online marketing tactics and conversion occurs on the website. Here, A and B are two versions of the same design, with slight changes founders as they found ready buyers in larger enterprise software companies. The number of to determine their effect. A/B testing is usually done in a controlled environment, with one variable being the control. A very simple example of A/B or split testing is to see the response and conversion rates when the call-to-action button is changed from red to green or vice versa.independent legacy ERP vendors shrank by hundreds during this era. The larger company's Multivariate testing saw the legacy installed base as a ready source of reliable cash flow from maintenance fees quickly upgraded to the new parent's system.

Multivariate testing is an essential component of CRO. A test that is applied to the various Key Performance Indicators, multivariate testing analyzes various elements by suggesting a number of variations and combinations. It determines which of these combinations would work best for a website and increases the conversion rate. The acquiring company's business plan was to cut the sales, marketing and development MVT uses statistical hypothesis testing on websites to make CRO authentic and reliable. With this technique, more than two variables of a website can be cost out of the legacy system's operating infrastructure. They would typically keep one or tested at once on the same page. Everything from landing page images, content and checkout forms to the font and color of texts can be tested with MVT. In short, it would be correct to say the MVT is synonymous to running multiple A/B tests at the same time. two key development and support personnel to keep the system afloat, then raise or hold Landing page maintenance fees, cutting out all other costs. With this strategy, profit margins on the legacy Landing page is an entry point for the visitors.

It is the page, which is shown in the search engine results when the user performs a search query. Once the system often exceeds 75%.user clicks on this page, the user enters the website and lands on the page called a landing page. This term refers to both organic and paid searches. In addition, other sources may direct visitors to the landing page, such as social media updates, emails, event invitations, etc.

The importance of a landing page is that it has great possibility of generating conversions. If your landing page resonates well with website visitors, it will result as it turned out, legacy customers did not always jump to the new owner's modern ERP in inspiring interest in your business and it will engage the visitors. Otherwise, poorly designed landing page will result in high bounce rate, and the visitors will unlikely return to your website.solution. First, there was no commonality between the old and the new system. From a training and implementation perspective, this meant starting over. Second, the new systems. Landing page has to be clear and direct in order to quickly engage the visitors. You should also carefully choose the design layout, with the company logo available. The information should be clearly visible, with a call-to-action button placed in a prominent place so that it attracts the attention of the visitor. Other lacked the deep, industry-specific functionality of the older system by giving up a lot of recommendations when it comes to optimizing your landing page include: developers overreached on the underlying system programming languages, middleware Include relevant visuals (for example, an image of the offer that can be claimed through the landing page)and databases, resulting in technical complexity and slow performance. Finally, many ERP companies increased support fees shortly after acquisition, alienating the legacy customer to many of these businesses provided like-for-like, cost-free license replacements to make up for these errors. The additional expense of reOnce you have a basic understanding of CRO, the next step is to delve into detail about the components that make up this idea, and the implementation was so extensive that clients started looking for new providers.

Statistics and calculations are frequently used. Conversion rate optimization, which is a crucial indicator of online marketing success, is elevated to a new level when users discover that they can purchase a completely new system from a different vendor with better specialist analysts that want to extract as much data as possible from this measure.

the business was profitable and cost less than what the new owners wanted. Today it is complete. It is therefore common to see a company that has decided to move away from its legacy system engage the CRO assessment, despite the fact that it is a straightforward process that is integrated with a number of other metrics. To make sure readers can easily understand the fundamentals, we shall examine the CRO computation in its most basic version. market and compare various vendors.

Conversion rate optimization is not a random evaluation, as was previously established. Data collection and processing.

The presence of a data warehouse is necessary for CRO. The platform that conducts this assessment first gathers data provided by customers and third party representatives. Once this data is gathered, it is processed to make sense. Relationships between variables on a website are developed and the strength of each is measured. A screening method is also used to drop irrelevant data before A/B testing and multivariate testing are used. Hypothesis

After adequate data is collected, a hypothesis is to be made. This hypothesis justifies why the change is needed and what the result of the change will be. Before starting this step, it should be kept in mind that the hypothesis must be measurable so that conclusions can be drawn.

Optimization goals

How much optimization do you want? What is the time duration for this improvement? How will it be tracked and measured? These are some important questions that website owners need to answer. Optimization goals lay the foundation of the CRO strategy. It should be remembered that optimization goals should strictly be in line with business goals because the former help in achieving the latter. The most basic optimization goal is to increase conversions. Later, companies have largely been acquired. In some cases, they have been bought and sold Next, an optimization strategy is put into effect. Once all the groundwork is done, this strategy will focus on achieving the goals set, and making the online marketing efforts of the company worthwhile.

more than once. More commonly, what we see in the marketplace today, is the larger ERP companies buying third-party technology to fill holes in their product line. Extended The numbers of functionality such as business intelligence, CRM, MES and WMS are being scooped up and

then attempted to integrate into the parent company's core system. Now for the quantitative part. The numbers related to CRO are derived by website analytics that are used on the internet. These analytical tools monitor traffic on the website and keep a track of how many customers report an action and those that only browse passively.

Therefore, to calculate the CRO, we will assume that the website is functioning normally and has all the necessary tools in place. For the most part, the acquiring companies have learned their lesson dramatically. To make use of the optimization strategy, you first need to know what the current conversion rate on your website is. Your current rate can be calculated using the following figures. raising support prices, but they still shortcut the integration of the companion technology

Total Conversions: This number is the actual quantity of customers who visited and reducing staff and service levels. The bolt-ons gradually assumed the status of "not your website" and recorded whatever action was required of them. Total Views: The total views is the number of people who have landed on your invention here or didn't work out like we planned" and are pushed to the backburner until the website, regardless of whether they took an action or not. This statistic would be the next big thing coming along. ideally be a bigger number than total conversions.

Using these figures, the conversion rate can be calculated using the formula:

CRO= (Total Conversions/Total Views) x100 Several early ERP system companies did have the foresight to re-platform their systems. So for instance, if the number of total views is 5000 and the number of total conversions is 50, the CRO turns out to be 1%. Today, these companies enjoy rich, industry-specific functionality and modern technology. While the calculation for CRO is simple, and so is the resulting answer, what does this number mean? What is the ideal CRO? How does this CRO compare to industry average? Is it enough to have a CRO of 1%? If not, how can this be improved?That enables advanced features like mobile apps and touch screen user interfaces. They are Making sense of the CRO, often the best choice for small and mid-market companies that require deep functionality like any other metric, the CRO percentage alone does not make much sense, nor is it useful to a business. Only when this number is compared, contrasted and gauged, against an ideal or a benchmark, does CRO start making some sense for online marketers.

Within this topic, two of the most important concepts related to CRO will be discussed. Without these, your website's CRO is only a figure that can neither be improved nor put to use.

The ideal CRO

Expert analysts are often hired to work on increasing a website's CRO to attract more business. When these experts compute the forum's conversion rate, the first question managers ask is whether this CRO is the best in the industry. How do you tell if it is?

The best or ideal percentage of conversion rate is often considered to be nonexistent. Since CRO varies from website to website, offer to offer and business to business, there really is not a benchmark to look at when it comes to improving this rate until a fixed point. The biggest reason why such a standard is an illusion lies within the formula used to calculate CRO.

Take a look at the equation again. Now consider this: If

you are using pay per click as an online marketing technique to promote your website, and for every click, you pay $1 in expenses, you could be recording an impressive CRO of 10%. However, if every action only leads to a profit of $2, the high CRO is not of much value, is it?

This is the reason why the CRO measure is relative for every industry and highly depends on the cost and profit structure your business follows. Consider another example. For instance, you have the following three scenarios in front of you: 100 visitors/day converting at 5% 500 visitors/day converting at 1% 5,000 visitors/day converting at 1%

Which one do you prefer? From the look of it, the first choice yields the highest CRO so it should definitely be the winner. However, according to experts, the third option is the one that is likely to reap the most results in terms of online marketing because having 5000 visitors daily and a 1% CRO means getting 50 conversions. However, with 100 visitors a day, as in the first option, only 5 sales are recorded. Therefore, it is obvious that defining the best or the ideal CRO is rather hard. It depends on various factors that are different for every website and every industry. Nonetheless, for comparison's sake, an average of 2%-3% CRO is often considered good for a company that is looked upon as reasonable by the market.

Metrics to help you understand CRO

Many rates and measures should be considered in conjunction to CRO when the time comes to analyze and draw a conclusion. Since these metrics support and clarify the conversion rate, they help in making sense of a percentage that would otherwise be hard to decipher.

The following four measures are all concerned with increasing viewership and revenue on websites. Hence, they help analysts in understanding what the CRO represents. The bounce rate

The bounce rate is a percentage representing the number of people who leave a website after viewing one page. This means that when passive surfers land on your home page, they do not find it attractive enough to go through in detail. They leave immediately, resulting in a high bounce rate – something that is highly important to address if you are to improve the CRO. Exit rate

While the bounce rate is for the entire website, the exit rate is particular for each page. A high exit rate for one page signifies the percentage of people who leave after viewing this page. This indicator gives analysts an insight into the last page a visitor viewed before leaving. Average time on site

Average time on site is the opposite of bounce rate. This metric represents how long viewers stay on your website on average. If the bounce rate is high, then the average time on site will be quite low, meaning that visitors are not staying long enough to perform an action. The measure of the average time on site is part of the engagement metric.

Average page views

The average page view indicates the number of pages viewed by browsers on average. This measure needs to be kept under check because a high average page view can signify two things. One, that visitors are engaged and find your website attractive, and second, that there is too much confusion in the conversion funnel on your webpage, which is why viewers are roaming around the forum without registering any action. Summary

Learning the basics about CRO demands that you understand its importance completely. Until you do, implementing strategies for conversion rate optimization will only be halfhearted. Website owners should pay attention to CRO for a number of reasons. Let us summarize these in three points:

Are Customer or Regulatory Requirements Keeping You From Obtaining

A high CRO results in better return on investment (ROI). Let us not forget that you are paying a hefty amount for large-scale internet advertising and for the New Business?upkeep of your website. If this investment yields low return, you are essentially incurring a low on marketing expenses. With a high CRO comes a possibility of higher sales, which make for an acceptable ROI. A high CRO is better than finding more viewers. While it may be easy to increase CRO, it is certainly an uphill task to get more viewers on your page. Securing new customers is not a straightforward task. How many times have you negotiated because intense marketing needs to be done for the latter. Therefore, working on improving CRO is more cost effective than increasing visitors to your page. A high CRO gives customers what they want. Remember, from the customer's perspective, a high CRO means finding the exact buttons, links, images, and a prospective contract to the finish line, only to discover that you are missing a critical content they want to see on their favorite website. Therefore, CRO is directly linked to customer loyalty and repeat purchases. piece of software necessary to obtain the new business? For example: The Basics of Search Engine Marketing If information is the superhighway then, the king of the road is the search engine. The short time in which the internet has become immensely accessible, search engines have become a useful tool. In fact, in the lives of the people, the idea of referring to a reference book or making phone calls to gather traceability functionality in the event of a recall information is an anathema. Therefore, the present and the coming generations rely on Bing, Yahoo!, Google, or any other search engine websites to collect • A large automotive manufacturer requires EDI in order to communicate knowledge and information. What happens is that the users enter any word in the search bar and the website returns with numerous search results almost instantly. Since this technology is now easily available, the library and the Yellow Page books are starting to look prehistoric. in order to accept the goods you produce for them The giant of the internet, Google, is presently so dominated that it performs more 3.5 billion searches per day. Bing and Yahoo! are the next to follow this giant search engine. It is the dream of every business that it shows up on top of the search result so that it gets the highest marketing through the internet. This is The automotive (TS), medical (FDA, 21 CFR Part 11) or ISO certification you are being done nowadays by promoting on Google and other search engines and in return, these businesses get closer to the top result. struggling to obtain requires functionality that your current software does not. If you are looking for a way to rank your webpage higher in the search result, the most basic thing you should do is to increase the number of websites that are connected to your web page. It is crucial to learn about the procedure to analyze the internet traffic via various ways. One way is that you open the

website's log files to find out how the viewer found your web page or website. It is important to know the significance of analyzing log files and traffic as these If this sounds familiar, you are not alone. Many manufacturers struggle to secure new customers (and ultimately grow their business) because they lack technical functionality. If the search engine marketing is done properly and regularly, it can be among the best ways to market your website and attract huge traffic towards it. It is common among the people to ignore the significance of a proper marketing strategy and executing the strategy regularly. This is an avoidable situation and found in a modern ERP system. Whether it is because you own a legacy ERP system that is must not be ignored as it holds huge benefits for your business.no longer being supported, you operate with a combination of multiple Excel spreadsheets To ignore the planning of a marketing strategy means that you are delaying the success of your business and certainly preventing it as well. Therefore, it is and QuickBooks or your software is too general or incompatible with manufacturing in vital that you have the understanding and the knowledge of the search engine marketing (SEM) and the different ways of using it. Basically, these methods provide much needed traffic to your business and promote it so that you earn a huge profit.order to land large, long-term customers, you need to consider upgrading to a more modern ERP solution.

Search engine marketing is the process of promoting your website, business or any content by using either paid methods, free methods or a combination of joining both the methods of the search engine optimization (SEO). This results in the increase of your content's ranking in the search engine result pages (SERPs). Short, yet really accurate, this is the basic job of search engine marketers. Many ERP vendors try to sell best of breed ERP as the ultimate solution. While integration Advantages of SEMof third-party programs into a core ERP system can work, it won't give you the end-to-end Among the many benefits that search engine marketing can provide, cost effectiveness is the major one. This can be demonstrated by using the pay-per-click traceability and visibility required by many customers and regulatory organizations. The methods. This method only charges you if a user clicks on your advertisement. Not only does this method let you feature the ads in the search engine result pages, where people can read the ad, but you only have to pay when the user clicks the ad. integration is typically fraught with challenges, such as duplicate data entry, information Next, if you learn the basics of the SEM, you will start looking for proven techniques and methods to increase your traffic. Every company has a longing for delays and silos, interface issues and customization expenses. huge traffic coming to their website. By properly using the SEM methods, you can increase the number of visits to your website so that your business flourishes. With the passage of time, SEM has out-struck almost every other method used for marketing and promotion. One of the biggest advantages SEM offers is The key to solving the aforementioned challenges is a comprehensive ERP solution. that the costs and expenses applied through the marketing are comparatively less than other means and methods of marketing. There are different SEM offering companies, which have different clients. Whichever company you choose, their costs would be less than what the other modes of marketing offer.

Comprehensive ERP is an end-to-end solution that covers every aspect of your business,

from ERP to MES, MRP, financials, order management, WMS, CRM and more. Another big advantage of SEM is that your advertisement would run twenty-four hours a day and seven days a week. All you have to do is choose the source system that makes every aspect of your business visible, traceable and incredible websites on the internet that you want to have your advertisement. If you wish to have the same days and hourly exposure through the other ways of efficient marketing, your budget would easily be blown out of the window.

Search engine marketing also allows complete control over your campaign, your audience, and the campaign costs. Finally, increased traffic means increased promotions, which further means increased sales. When an increased number of people start getting to know about Let's look at some of the customer and regulatory challenges that are solved with your company or any content on the website, many of these people will start converting into customers and clients. It is highly effective if you execute an email list building strategy.comprehensive ERP:

It is important that whatever you decide should be friendly to your budget at hand. What this means is that if you do not have a large sum of money available, paid advertisement methods should not be considered as an option. Rather the less expensive method, SEO, should be considered. However, search engine Serial and Lot Tracking:

From the raw materials in your warehouse, to the work optimization has disadvantages as well. Conclusively, after filtering out the techniques that fall under your budget, the pros and cons of each method should be weighed and the best one should be chosen so that you are comfortable with.center they were processed on, all the way to the shipping truck, comprehensive Internet marketing: search engine marketing serial and lot tracking allows you to follow the lifecycle of every piece, part, box As mentioned above, search engine marketing is a type of internet marketing that promotes websites by enhancing their visibility in the search result of the and pallet in your company automatically.

search engines (Google, Yahoo!, etc.). Search engine marketing has two categories.

Paid advertising

This type of search engine marketing uses paid reach to attract the visitors. The paid marketing methods (such as the pay-per-click method) provide fast

results. However, they are expensive and one must always take a look at the budget before choosing any method.

Search engine optimization Search engine optimization (SEO) uses so-called organic reach so that the website or any content of the client is adjusted and rewritten in order to increase the visibility of that content in the search engine search results.

Paid advertising results are displayed at the top of the SERP, above the organic search results. Paid results can also be displayed on the side, and in the bottom of SERP. The workings of internet marketing can be summarized into four categories through which the websites get optimized:

Keyword analysis and its research

This step is further categorized into three steps. First, you need to make sure that the website can be included in the search engines according to the proper order. Next step is finding the most relevant and accurate keyword of the website that can sum up the content of the website in just a single word or a phrase. Finally, use that keyword on the website in such a way that it will show up high in the search result and attract an increased amount of internet user traffic.

CHAPTER NINE

Quality and Risk Management:

Mitigate risk, adhere to strict certification Progress on the effect on keyword research and analysis is known as the search perception impact. This describes the known impact of a search result, of any brand, on the perception of the consumer. This includes site indexing, meta tags, titles, and the focused keyword. Since searching online for something is the requirements and maintain customer compliance requests with a suite of quality first step to becoming a customer, the search perception impact carves the impression of a brand for each person. Popularity of the website and saturation management products, including certificates of conformance, document control, SPC, quality audit, MRB, ECO, CAR and PLM. Also known as the amount of website's visibility in the search engines, website saturation can be examined by the number of pages of the website available in the search engines and the number of backlinks that the website has. In this method, it is a requirement that a keyword should be present in the pages, which the people can search for, as this would ensure a high rank in the search result. Many of the search engines make use of the link popularity to rank the

different results. A comprehensive labeling application with features specific to your manufacturing industry can help you create customer back-end tools, specific labels with individualized barcodes, print different sized or colored labels on the fly for quick part identification, handle multiple label types. These tools give data on the visitors of the website and the site itself measures the success of that website. HTML validators and web analytic tools are the common tools used in this step. These tools can be as simple as counting the traffic that is arriving at a website, to tools that deal with log files and to complex (product, container, shipping and mix-load), eliminate mismatched items, utilize tools that are based upon page tagging. These back-end tools deliver the information related to conversions as well. Large companies often combine the label sequencing capabilities and accurately print the correct label every time. usage of several types of tools, so they could be using tools that analyze log files, tag-based investigative tools, and transition-based tools. The validators check for any invisible parts of the sites, highlight the possible problems and usage issues and then ensure that the site meets the requirements EDI: of the W3C. It is a good idea to use more than one spider simulator or HTML validator for these purposes, as each of these reports highlight and test different areas of the website. Who is tool With an Electronic Data Interchange (EDI) module, you can easily translate

incoming files directly into your ERP solution and then automatically generate

outgoing files for transfer back to your customers and suppliers. Embedded EDI

This tool discloses the owners of the website. These tools play an important role in providing valuable information regarding the copyright issues and trademark issues of the website. also automatically alerts you to any changes in deliverables, quantities or due dates for up-to-the-minute order accuracy.

This is a method that involves the search engine companies to charge fees for including the website on their top search results. This method is also known as paid inclusion and sponsored listing. The products, that are to be advertised, show up on the separate ad-bar of the search engine, or show up at the top of the pages of the search engine results. Customer or compliance challenges from a lack of modern software tools do not have search engine website allowing paid inclusions only, they benefit a little from success. Search engines like Yahoo! support the stance of providing mix keep you from securing new business. With a comprehensive ERP solution, you will have paid inclusions to the SEO and SEMs.traceable and transparent quality processes throughout your organization.

The paid method used in search engine marketing includes advertising with search engine advertising programs, that allow users to create sponsored results that are to be displayed in the search engine result pages.

Each search engine has some sort of advertising program, with Google AdWords and Bing Ads being the two most commonly used, due to a large number of searches conducted through these two search engines.

When it comes to paid advertising, search engines offer several types of ads, which often include:

Pay-per-click advertising (PPC)

This type of advertising is also called cost-per-click (CPC) advertising and it means that you pay any time someone clicks on your ad shown in the search engine result pages. This type of advertising is most commonly used by the advertisers as it requires payment only after your ad has been able to attract visitors to click on it.

Cost-per-thousand impressions (CPM)

This advertising model is focused on the number of impressions, i.e. the number of times that your ad has been shown. Using this type of advertising you pay for each set of one thousand impressions.While the text ads appearing in the search engines result pages are the most common type of search engine advertising, there are other ad formats available, which might help you with different types of campaign goals. These include:

Text ads Ad extensions Images Mobile text or image ads App promotion ads Videos Product listing ads The position of search engine marketing today. Every business believes and trusts in the potential of SEM. Since the previous decade, growth in search engine marketing has been immense, beating every other industry. As a large number of internet users keep utilizing the internet as their primary option, in finding the right company for their needs and wants, SEM will continue to prevail as the forefront leaders of marketing.

Businesses have realized that the acquisition of cost is acceptable through SEM, causing an effective increase in the resources through savings in the marketing budgets.

In case you have missed out in making a proper and formal search engine marketing strategy in the first place, or you have left some filler in the marketing budget used for SEM purpose, it is suggested that you rethink the strategy and consider the benefits that would lead your business and company on the mountains of success. All of this is essential, as the business needs to create a strong effective presence in the eyes of the search engines, especially Google. Carefully look into all the requirements and updates given by the search engines and organize a strategy accordingly.

Paid reach is a frequently used method in the marketing strategy by a lot of companies nowadays. However, the search engine advertising programs are available to anyone, and they have become an important tool in developing and growing small businesses as well. In a modern

Business world where being positioned at the top of the result pages has become a signal of success, you need to do your best to increase the visibility of your website in relation to the keywords that are associated with your business.

Since using organic reach, i.e. SEO, can be long-term effort with lots of obstacles on the way, paid reach has become a simple alternative, an easy solution to get at the top instantly. Besides being ranked at the top of the search results, paid advertising also has other benefits, which include: Attract more clients

. The main benefit of search engine advertising is the possibility to reach more clients, which are the users you would not be able to attract using organic reach only. This helps you expand your market as your business becomes visible to the new customers.

Target the ads

The possibility of targeting the users is a huge benefit of advertising program, as you will be able to completely set the criteria according to which the ads will be displayed in the search engines. Google AdWords allows the following targeting options:5. Auditing ERP for Manufacturing Fit and Functionality Keyword targeting Location and language targeting Device targeting

Does the following describe your current ERP situation?

Using paid advertising program allows you to be in charge of your campaign, by setting up the budget and the time period that budget is to be spent. This way, you will only spend the budget you have planned to assign to this type of campaign. As the campaign runs, you will be able to analyse the budget spending and to adjust it accordingly.

Track conversions

Each advertising program offers a platform for managing the campaign, which also provides the features for evaluating the performance of the In other words, your ERP system may be lacking software fit and functionality. Software campaign. Therefore, you can track conversions and make sure that your campaign is really successful. You can also monitor traffic and analyze the functionality relates to the modules, tools and features available to meet the needs of your business, such as finance and accounting, inventory and purchasing, production execution, arehouse management and customer relationship management. How effectively the modules' functionalities satisfy your needs is referred to as software fit. In a larger sense, search engine marketing is a subcategory of online advertising that also encompasses search engine optimization. unique business models and procedures, as mentioned. The earlier list, which contains both organic and paid search results, can be identical between two ERP systems. Organic results react differently but are totally based on search engine features. Finding the optimal optimization requires both functionality and fit, but sponsored search results require employing advertising tools like Google AdWords and Bing Ads.

Both should be carefully considered as an ERP solution.

SEM frequently uses Google AdWords or Bing Ads for sponsored advertising. Pay-per-click marketing is advantageous to advertisers because it allows clients to contact the business directly with only one click. When referring to sponsored advertisements, advertising, article submissions, and an SEO functional audit are crucial considerations. A keyword analysis is carried out for both SEO and SEM. It is not necessary for them to be completed simultaneously, though.

In a contemporary manufacturing setting, conventional wisdom holds that three information technology components—SEO, SEM, and cloud computing—are crucial to growth and corporate success. In order to be able to analyze earlier practices, upgrading should be done frequently.

Software for customer relationship management (CRM), manufacturing execution systems, and enterprise resource planning (ERP). While this conventional wisdom is unquestionably accurate, it can also be misleading because terminology like ERP, MES, and CRM are general in nature and frequently serve as stand-ins for more specific lists of the capabilities required to improve a manufacturing operation.

Search engine traffic is well-known to be highly focused. This is mostly due to the prospective repeat customers who look at your B2B offerings through various search engines. Consumers are totally inclined to examine your marketing messages and adverts that align with their online beliefs because they are looking for services and items on their own. There are currently features. Make sure to take into account the fact that no other marketing channel can provide a more qualified and effective prospect than this when assessing new or existing ERP functionality. In conclusion, the following characteristics set search engine marketing apart from other forms of promotion and advertising: User-generated behaviors that the software provider has loosely included.

Search engine marketing is the end consequence of user conclusions as a whole. Visitors from various directories and search engines chose to check out your company on their own initiative rather than looking at any of your rivals. One of the reasons why people utilize the internet

While integrating outside programs can be successful, the Challenges like repeated data entry, information delays and silos, interface problems, and Non-intrusive behavior customization costs are frequently present in processes. The advantages of a native ERP solution are numerous, and they include Always remember that SEM is a non-intrusive marketing strategy. Consumer behavior is interrupted by the majority of adverts, both offline and online, which are always visible and traceable into every area of your organization. For instance, visitors may come across various pop-ups and real-time speed and responsiveness that are employed as adverts while browsing the internet. However, while people are reading a newspaper, the advertisements section takes over their thoughts and compels them to stop reading in order to look at the ad. Internet users actively look for your information and services through SEM. and You can use the list below two ways: to examine your current ERP system for the production of the goods that were stated in the advertisement they viewed. The advertisements that users view in search results are pertinent to the user's search query and are intended to meet that demand. Therefore, search engine ads are useful and functional or to reduce your choice of a new system to two or three finalists rather than being invasive and creating a distraction. Which ERP system makes or misses the cut is ultimately decided by the Fit Acid Test that is discussed later in this document.

Since the beginning of the last decade, the internet has grown quickly. Everything is done with God's blessing, from online purchasing to connecting with people abroad. using the internet. Due to important internet components like search engine optimization and search engine marketing, search engines have helped businesses succeed in their specialized industries. The effective method of promoting and advertising firms on the internet is search engine marketing (SEM). It is critical for firms to use these strategies in order to increase success in their operations. If marketing is done correctly, SEM has a number of benefits.One must never delay a marketing strategy, as it is a known fact that right marketing brings much needed success for every business. Every search engine has its own requirements when speaking about SEM. Google is the current king of search engines, leaving Bing and Yahoo! behind.

CHAPTER TEN

There are different methods and ways to earn high ranks in search engines.

Every search engine requires different SEM techniques as well. You should follow all the guidelines and recommendations in order to ensure success for your business.

The Basics of Social Media Marketing Financial Accounting Details General ledger, fixed asset, payables receivables (cash application and collections), cash management, budgeting, costing until just a few years ago, social media was known as a domain for school-going kids. It was looked upon as a set of forums that were used by Order Processing youngsters to socialize, share personal details, and discuss the topics of their interest. With parents wary and instructors strict about its usage, what Order entry, credit checking, pricing, available/capable to promise, we today proudly call our business partners, were previously considered a nuisance. The sudden rise to power of social media had every business and for that matter, adults, taken aback. With a successful business website, most Material Resource Planning

Production planning, resource planning, scheduling, inventory online companies were happily dealing with customers on a daily basis from a single touchpoint. However, when social media roared its head high, the possibility of unlimited touchpoints baffled even the most expert of businessmen. control, purchasing

Today, business without social media is not even an option. The effect this channel has on how information is received, perceived and shared is Supply Chain management Planning, supplier scheduling, product configurator, purchasing, profound. So much so, that even if a business wants to stay out of social media, it just cannot bear the risk of losing all those customers who are present on it. This move, however, has not taken the channels themselves by surprise. Electronic Data Over the years leading up to this change, social media companies made sure they provide everything on their websites that was desired by people. Electronic interfaces for customer and suppliers, POs, shipping Interchange (EDI) notifications, invoicesMeeting friends, engaging in conversations, looking for businesses, finding restaurants or even recommendations for the best products, you name it and it is there. Therefore, the pull towards social media increased tremendously when the services they offered started to expand.

Warehouse Management Receiving, put away, picking and packing One such service that channels like Facebook, Twitter and LinkedIn started to provide was customized and intimate pages to represent a business and connect with its customers. Using this as a springboard, early adopters of social media started promoting their products, engaged customers in Business Intelligence Standard reports, report writing, ad hoc queries, summary 61 Reporting & Dashboards dashboards and alerts Since social media offer a direct and personal platform to connect with a company, customers are more keen on seeing a business on these forums rather than visiting a website which is why social media has allowed so many benefits to modern businesses, regardless the type of the activity and the target audience in question. Product definitions version control and exchange master data focused on defining. It is estimated that over 70% of internet users are present on at least one social network, which means that a majority of users can in fact be how to make a product reached through social media. Production schedule, work orders, production requirements,

CHAPTER ELEVEN

What is Social media marketing (SMM) received from EPR to make optimal use of resources.

Social media marketing (SMM) has become a buzzword in today's world. With the usage of social media at an all-time high, successful businesses Production Dispatch have shifted quite a chunk of their promotional load to online platforms that are visited by thousands of users on a daily basis. No marketing and distribution of batches, runs and work orders, adjustment to execution promotional strategy is now complete without a sizable budget and room for social media marketing. What is SMM? unanticipated conditions. Checks on resources and informing Social media marketing is a type of online marketing that is geared towards social websites and forums. Such marketing efforts are made to other systems about the progress of production processes to achieve communication and branding goals because each of these is at the heart of a promotional campaign. In other words, when a business has Process Monitoring set up a page on social websites with all its details and products, it wants to attract attention and traffic to it. SMM is the method employed to do so. Collection of process data, equipment status, material lot Social media marketing has many similarities with search marketing. The defining factor about search marketing is the discovery and realization of information and production logs in a data historian. Performance new stories, ideas and news. With SMM in full swing, the same can be achieved when businesses put up new and interesting stories, catchy images and content that is full of needed information. analysis of raw production data. WIP overviews, period production performance, overall equipment effectiveness or any other Hence, SMM is only another form of search marketing that has been introduced ever since social media appeared. With a refreshing take on the performance indicator. Track and trace. Registration and retrieval latter, SMM has developed new ways to market the same products, using channels of communication that are visited by the audience more than any search engine website. of information that

presents a complete history of lots, orders and equipment Therefore, content creation is at the heart of every SMM campaign. Companies looking to market themselves on social media create interesting content that they hope users will like and share, generating a stream of communication. This results in, what experts call, the electronic parameters that can feed a statistical process control module

Digitizing, Audit and Digitizing log data with edit lock, also pulling data from the QualityInterchange (EDI) supervisory control and data acquisition system into the common databank. Audit utilities to evaluate and document performance and events. Statistical quality control tools word of mouth (eWoM). The eWoM includes any statement, perception, comment or like and dislike generated for the content posted on social forums. This is taken to be a signal of approval and recommendation, or disapproval in case the reaction to the product or service is negative.

Social media enabled these comments to be widely accessible to social media users, which is why this can be both an advantage or a disadvantage for a business struggling to create its reputation.

Once the stream of communication has spread far and wide, a result that is imminent when using social media, the marketing efforts of the business are trusted by the audience because they seem to be coming from independent third parties instead of the business itself. Hence, such marketing becomes 'earned' and not 'paid', something that resonates very well with the ever-so-suspicious customer of today. Social media platforms Social media is a broad term. Within this broad definition of social websites, we can distinguish social forums that are very different from each other, and so the way businesses are marketed on them is starkly different as well. SMM has two main outlets, one being social media websites and secondly we have smartphone devices.

CRM Details; The number of social media websites on the internet today is surprising. From several that existed some 10 years ago, hundreds have sprung up Customer Information To attract viewers belonging to different lifestyles, having particular interests. Before a social media marketer targets marketing efforts on an online Company and contact information, sales history, contact history, forums, they need to be fully aware of the various platforms that exist in this category. Open and closed opportunities Facebook Prospect Information Company and contact information, contact history, open and Facebook is one of the oldest and the most popular social networks around. The platform has a very casual and upbeat feel to it, where users have closed opportunities to interact, look for products and services and recommend the same to the list of friends and family they have added. Pipeline Management Ability to report of the value and likelihood of open opportunities

Marketing Campaigns Ability to create and track email campaigns Marketing on Facebook has proved to be quite effective. Over the years, many businesses have sprung up solely because they made a Customer Service

Company and contact information, open calls, closed calls, Facebook fan page and started to market their products and services. Therefore, SMM on Facebook has led to the growth of online businesses Managementthat have become successful even without any brick and mortar presence. metrics, ability to track service calls by issue type.

On a particular Facebook fan page, a business can use different techniques to optimize the page in order to appease visitors and create a fan following. Facebook also offers a paid advertising service to businesses that allow them to choose the image and text that goes in the Technology Details Advertisement. Using the pay-per-click strategy, a business is charged whenever the ad is clicked on.

Single Database All subsystems run from one database and one native body of codeThis social media marketing platform is all about gaining a solid base of followers. Twitter is a social website that lets users post or 'tweet' small

updates related to new product launches, sales, and upcoming events or simply wish followers a good day to ignite a thread of conversation. The Real-Time' information flows through the system in real time. There are no

batch updates ability to Manage Multiple Total cross-location visibility of all information in real time Locations.

The entire purpose behind social media marketing with Twitter is to initiate dialogue with your fans. Because many businesses become alienated from their market, Twitter is present to counter just that. The more you communicate, the better you will connect with the Ability to Scale Users.

Ability to maintain performance within a broad user, load and market. In addition, Twitter helps you provide quick replies, which can help you improve your customer support. Like Facebook, Twitter also allows companies to advertise through this social media platform. storage parameters, Google+ Deployment Software licenses purchased and deployed on company premises.

A strong competitor in the social media market, Google+ has been customized so that it provides many new features for SMM that other Software licenses purchased and deployed at third-party data websites do not. The possibility to integrate several Google services, such as Google Maps, is perfect for integrating those into the center. SaaS or Cloud software rented from a software provider promotion of your business. Google+ also has a fun and casual approach to sharing pictures, videos and links. The website also has a feature called Google+ circles that lets businesses segment their entire market into various groups.

Fit Acid Test(s): Once you have audited the functionality and fit with the tools above, ask your team the following questions: "What makes our business unique? What makes us consistently profitable?" It may be changing colors on the fly, absolute cost control, aSMM can then be targeted to each group separately. For instance, if you want to offer discounts only to selected fans, who have made the most purchases, Google+ circles will be useful to you. Similarly, Google+ communities allow groups of people to communicate and unique pricing plan or something else entirely. Every business has a "secret sauce" that is interact through a single community focused on particular interest. an essential business strategy. Define that strategy and determine with absolute certainty Hangout is another versatile feature of this website. With Hangout, a business can host online video conferences and tutorials to keep that the ERP systems you are evaluating can implement it perfectly. users interested, to introduce or promote a new product or service, to announce events, etc.

Perform this simple acid test, determine the function and fit, and that your top vendor's LinkedIn is a professional social website that attracts business people from various industries. This forum is perfect for initiating a choice of deployment options. Chances are very high you will pick the right finalists.

conversation with people from the same industry and post content rich articles that will be understood by like-minded people. There are many features like LinkedIn groups, that help you segment the target market and attract them with different content, and LinkedIn profile, where customers can give testimonials and in effect, recommend your business to others.

YouTube YouTube needs no introduction. Being the number one channel for video communication, businesses have taken advantage of the various audio and visual features of YouTube to create content rich videos and target them at customers and fans. YouTube videos can also be posted on Facebook and Twitter to double the SMM effect. How-to videos are a tried and trusted way to gain a following and appear in the top ranks on the website.

Foursquare

Foursquare is a location based social media website. It is an ideal way for local businesses to register and claim a location spot, where customers can later check in, when they visit this restaurant, café, salon etc. The check in status is then visible to friends and family who find this enough encouragement to try the new service.

CHAPTER TWELVE

How to Increase Plant Capacity Without Adding Resources.

Moreover, these businesses can offer discounts and reward points for a certain number of check-ins. Being available as an app on smartphones, customers can post real-time reviews if they like the services, thus spreading positive word of mouth. As the manufacturing industry continues to grow, manufacturers are experiencing a welcomed increase in demand. While optimistic about the future of the manufacturing. The usage of platforms is also affected by their compatibility on mobile devices. Smartphones and tablets have replaced the traditional desktops industry, many companies are exercising caution when it comes to expansion. This prudent and laptops in the last decade or so. These mobile devices are now fitted with technologies that enable users to browse through the internet. Look attitude has prompted many to ask, "How can I grow capacity without adding floor space, through social content, pick advertisements and communicate with friends on various forums. With these devices, does social media marketing has equipment or personnel?"definitely found an avenue to attract attention and retain it using efforts that are customized and tailored for smartphones and tablets.

New applications are available every few months that let smartphone users explore social media content with a lot of convenience.

There are two common routes manufacturers take when faced with a surge in demand. The first is to maintain the status quo with current business processes and operations while adding new work centers, employees and square footage to handle the increase. The alternate defining social media strategy is a process that is quite unique for each company, as each company has distinctive goals and the methods that route is to dial up all existing resources as efficiently as possible first prior to expanding are to be used in the realization of those goals. There are many steps in a social media marketing strategy that need to be followed in order to ensure the success of the strategy. With the second option, the ultimate goal would be 100% utilization of what you already have. While every social website has a plan of its own when it comes to using its space, the general process followed by online marketers remains the same. have before adding on more personnel and equipment. In terms of these steps, traditional marketing and online marketing, both may have a lot of commonalities. However, in no way is one exchangeable for the other because the dynamics of marketing changes as soon as it is taken to the virtual world. tuned plant that finishes one job and immediately begins the next, with the proper tools, You must have an idea by now that social media is an expansive field. No longer does this term refer to only Facebook and Twitter. A lot of other operators and materials prepped and ready to deploy. How can you make the right job, websites have entered the market, making marketing rather challenging. Therefore, it is imperative that an online marketer starts with a plan in mind. with the right tools and right quantities all flow together at the right time? Some basic elements of planning include answering these questions: Who is my audience? What do I want to promote? How will I promote it? What tools will I use? How long will the campaign be active? What does the market prefer to see in terms of advertising? When you answer all of these questions, you will have a list of goals, tasks and resources you are going to use when developing a social media

The answer is a comprehensive ERP and MES solution capable of automating your shop floor. While integration of third-party programs into a core ERP system can work, it is fraught with challenges, such as duplicate data entry, information delays and silos, interface Without having concrete goals, a social media marketing campaign will be incomplete, indecisive and highly vague. The goals vary depending on the type of business you want to promote, but there are some goals that are commonly defined by online marketers, and those include: to do content optimization, get interest by creating quality articles and promoting them on social media.

Also, remember no matter which platform you use, being present and involved in the target audience's life is what makes them remember you. The secret to expanding capacity is to have an all-encompassing solution that addresses every raising conversion rates Increasing brand awareness levels driving more people to websites establishing communication between all areas of your organization, including ERP, MES, MRP, financials, order management, WMS, and CRM.a chasm between the business and Because of this single point of contact, every part of your company is accessible and traceable for customers. fostering positive brand associations fostering a feeling of community via superior customer service

Leveraging of a platform

Where Can I Initially See the Biggest Capacity Increase? As was already stated, there are a lot of social networks available to online marketers, but it is neither feasible nor cost-effective to be present on every single one of them on the shop floor module of an all-encompassing ERP solution with the fastest ROI. The platform that will help you reach your target audience and thus be most productive among those that are available is the process monitoring package. By immediately linking to high-value and efficient work centers when implementing social media marketing strategy.

The most well-known social media sites for SMM have been thoroughly covered above. Online, there are numerous other sites like Yelp, Instagram, Reddit, Pinterest, etc. manufacturing tools at the sensor and Programmable Logic

Controller (PLC) levels Every feature available on these platforms is unique and serves a certain marketing objective. The platform you employ to gather process parameters and promptly transmit that data to an ERP solution for your social media campaign will therefore rely on your objectives and how frequently your target market utilizes the particular social website.

The process monitoring tools will significantly increase productivity and efficiency after analysis. For instance, if your only goal is to inform your target audience with regular updates like discounts, sales, etc

Twitter is the ideal forum for this. Your business's efficiency rises as a result of process monitoring since two-way communication takes place in real time. On the other hand, Facebook and Google+ offer RP alternatives if you want to carry out a big SMM using images, videos, and content optimization. A few advantages of process monitoring are as follows:

The next stage is to carry out your pre-made plan after choosing one or more social media channels on which to concentrate your social media activities. Create a brief, captivating advertisement that will go viral if your marketing plan relies on paid advertising. Gather all significant production-related variables, if you like, including temperature, pressure, dimensions, weight, thickness, fill rate, etc.

Create interest by producing high-quality articles and marketing them on social media for correct content optimization. Auto-populate the collected data into the ERP's SPC module for better decision-making.

Also keep in mind that, regardless of the medium you choose, engaging with and being present in the lives of your target audience is what will help them remember you. Therefore, even if nothing new is happening on your end, constantly stay updated with regular posts. Additionally, using both free and paid marketing strategies is the greatest way to ensure that news of your campaign spreads widely. Hence, always stay in touch with regular posts even if there is nothing new happening on your end. Moreover, making use of free, as well as paid marketing techniques, is the best way to make sure word of your campaign reaches far and wide.

Monitor and control

When you advertise on Facebook, the website gives you access to monitor the success of the campaign with the help of bar charts, pie graphs and line graphs. You are told how many people viewed your advertisement, how many clicked on it and who shared your status update with others. Such insights make monitoring and controlling the various aspects of SMM quite easy.

Changes to the campaign can also be made if you know how well social media users are receiving it. For instance, if you observe that your page likes were more with your previous ad, it is a clear sign that the new one needs some improvement. Changing small aspects like placement and airtime can significantly alter results. • Track whether a job is running too fast or too slow, then review your operations Besides monitoring paid social media campaigns, you can use web analytics tools to monitor traffic from social media, or you can use tools that record your social media activity, and enable you to evaluate the performance of your strategy.to ensure part quality, adjusting your upcoming jobs on the schedule accordingly Some social networks, such as Facebook, provide their own insights, which enable page owners to assess the performance of the activity on the:

• Catch and respond to rejects and parts trending out of specification page. Some of the data included in the Facebook insights are page likes, post reach, engagement, etc. as they occur, not hours later when you receive a production report

• Increase accountability throughout the organization since unscheduled Google+ also offers insights. Although there is less data, it still helps you evaluate the visibility and engagement on your Google+ page. downtime, employee labor, parts produced and more are fully tracked as they occur Benefits of social media marketing The bottom line is that you can't hide from real-time process monitoring - it always exposes. There are many perceptions and schools of thought regarding social media marketing. For some it is a fad that they hope will 'die' down soon, the truth about what is actually happening on your shop floor. while others feel it is a learning curve, of which you should be taking advantage. Nonetheless, it is unanimously agreed that social media marketing is in the spotlight, and it has become a part of modern business. Hence, it makes sense to benefit from it. One successful manufacturer in Germantown, Wisconsin uses his process monitoring Compared to traditional marketing, SMM yields many benefits that should be cashed in on because marketing is a constant, no matter which module to run a completely lights-out manufacturing facility 24/7. From the central material

handling system to the automated box conveyor system, all parts are run without human Extensive surveys and studies carried out by experts in SMM, like Hubspot and Social Media Examiner, reveal some convincing statistics about interaction. This lights-out facility is only achievable with a comprehensive ERP system online marketing in general and social media marketing in particular. One set of results showed that a significant 90% of marketers said that social media is important to their businesses. 63% of marketers are using social media for 6 hours or more and 39% for 11 or more hours weekly that allows the manufacturing staff to monitor and schedule all production from an off-site Therefore, social media marketing is an effort that will result in multiple benefits for your business, and some of those benefits include the following: facility. Thanks to automatic alerts customized to trigger when certain parameters are not met, the employees know immediately if problems arise. When marketers pitch their ideas and products on social media websites, they expose their business to an audience that they would have otherwise missed. From the young to the old, every age group is now on social websites and prefers to do product searches on these platforms. Production monitoring tools also allow you to create a second (or third) shift if demand Hence, when this audience sees your services and marketing efforts, it starts to recognize you. Eventually, by interacting with your social continues to increase. Without an automated tracking and monitoring system, an additional followers, you establish a relationship of recognition and loyalty, and this will have a positive influence on your branding and promotion. Making use of the reach of the internet shift would mean a shortage of senior staff members. You can either have fewer eyes on There is no other marketplace as resourceful and expansive as the internet. Moreover, there are hardly any websites that are more visited than the floor or have less experienced employees working the shift, neither of which are ideal.

For example, one successful manufacturer uses the process monitoring module in its comprehensive ERP solution to run its work centers in cells, with six machines to each cell. Rather than have six operators, one for each machine, the manufacturer uses the software to employ only one supervisor to oversee all six of the machines in his cell. With automatic Increase conversion alerts that tell him if the job is having difficulty or if parts are trending out of specification, With every post, picture and update, you increase the chance of converting more passive viewers to active customers. In the physical,the traditional model of one operator per work center is no longer required. world, getting in touch with your market every few minutes is not only costly, it is literally impossible.

The Areas in the Software That Increase Demand Capacity: Without SMM, the people visiting your website are either those who have repeatedly purchased from you before or those who manage In addition to process monitoring, there are many other tools that can increase capacity. to find your website in the search engine result pages. On social media, however, every new update is liked or shared, which increases For example, some systems offer finite scheduling and dispatch list tools that automatically the chances of attracting those who had never even heard about your business and who would not be able to find your business on their own. analyze which operators and work centers are the most efficient. The software answers the Reduced cost of marketing question: of all your tools, people and machines, which ones run the best for this particular SMM is cheaper compared to traditional means of promotion. Where does it take more than a few hundred dollars to erect a billboard with a job? The system then smartly loads your work centers based on historical performance data,your products on it, it only takes $10-$15 for a small business to create an advertisement on Facebook and no charge at all for creating ensuring that you are optimally using your assets.

Making us of different Methods

You can run optimal order sizes in addition to using optimal equipment. Automated social networks enable the use of various content formats, enabling you to develop distinctive marketing plans to support ERP solutions that build appropriate production order batch amounts through minimum and maximum for your business. You can exchange text postings, pictures, and videos; arrange online contests and promotions; and publish questions and solicit feedback, among other things. To maximize your use of social media, there are numerous options to customize your strategy. 'Multiple of' designations, run sizes, and time fences to prevent pointless teardowns Everyone may access it, and it resets while enhancing production runs.

Every business, regardless of size or industry, has access to social networks. You can build profiles or pages on social networks for free, and all you need to invest in managing your social media accounts and doing social media marketing is time.

You have a strategy in mind. Summary Social media marketing is a cutting-edge and imaginative alternative to traditional and physical corporate advertising. Regardless of how fresh or how old your business is, a great SMM strategy may do wonders to increase fan following and the conversion rate for your website. Your organization must consequently, if it hasn't already, make the social leap. You may give your business a new appearance and feel by keeping in mind the rules and variables that govern this marketing plan. You will also have the ability to explore how social interaction and communication can aid in brand promotion.

CHAPTER THIRTEEN

The Basics of Search Engine Optimization

Many Bills of Material (BOMs) found in ERP software are cookie cutter templates that fit only Introduction one or two manufacturing processes. But manufacturers today are multi-process companies. There is nothing worse than creating a website but failing to reach its potential users and customers. This dilemma plagues a large chunk of and needs the fields and tools to handle multi-execution manufacturing. Accurate, process website search marketing industry today; this is where SEO comes in. SEO is the essential practice of drastically improving the performance of specific BOMs allowing the automated schedulers to do their jobs correctly. your website by attracting increased inbound traffic from organic, non-paid search engine result pages or SERPs. SEO, in today's world, is a vital concept. However, it is often subjected to various misconceptions, and unrealistic ideas about what it can and One way to increase capacity is with manufacturing-specific BOMs and routing workflows cannot achieve. There are various forms of SEO that are in practice today and these include white hat, black hat and gray hat search engines that offer 30-plus different manufacturing types, with fields and features specific to each optimization. These primarily differentiate based on the kind of techniques that are used. Some are used while functioning within the bounds of process. Whether you produce by weight, length or pieces, or through continuous or batch permissible rules and regulations while others work by being in direct conflict with the given guidelines production, the BOM should speak your language. The software should also offer multi-level

It is very important to realize the real-time results of SEO and not to be confused or swayed by unrealistic ideas of gains. SEO requires a great deal of investment and time. It is a lengthy and an expensive process and it is not suitable for all websites. This is of great significance, knowing BOMs, display equipment and labor requirements and contain the flexibility to schedule when to use SEO and when to use other mediums for rankings. processes that are work center, assembly line, application based or a combination of many SEO industries are extremely competitive today. Search engines, owing to the past manipulations, have now resorted to using extensively complex and strict algorithms for ranking, and for effective SEO, it is important to conform to these algorithms. Significant search engines like Google, Yahoo! and Bing now incorporate these algorithms and work along the strict rules of non-disclosure in order to avoid breaches in the security and the dangers of carrying too much on-hand inventory are high. But with a comprehensive ERP solution, just-in-time material principles are built into your daily practices, thereby lowering your inventory levels and minimizing production costs because materials are only Search Engine Optimization or SEO refers to the most essential and the most crucial aspect of establishing your website's visibility on significant search engines, which function along the ordered when needed.

Intelligent material resource planning (MRP) tools, such as safety stock features that automatically generate purchase orders when common inventory items run low, increase your inventory turn rate, ensuring you keep just the minimum quantity lines of non-payment, and natural search results. This is in contrast to the paid-for ads that show up under search listings. With the advent of time, search engines are becoming increasingly sensitive to content quality and relevance of the information provided. Unethical stuffing of keywords, plagiarism, and buying links is rigorously barred and penalized.

A common cause of job resets and rescheduling of production orders due to delayed Search engine optimization is based on a few, specifically required elements, which should, under all circumstances, be taken care of in order to communicate between the change in an order and the shop floor. With an Electronic, achieve true SEO. SEO includes the fourtier concept of, on-page SEO, SEO content writing, and code optimization, and link building. It boils down to providing a good user experience, natural and well-written content, natural inclusion of keywords in the main body of the text and the overall Data Interchange (EDI) module, you gain accurate, up-to-the-minute order accuracy. With an ERP solution, you can automatically and immediately recognize the change. Your ERP Search engine optimization, or SEO, functions along four vital processes or elements: solution can check for changes every hour or every minute automatically, based on your

CHAPTER FOURTEEN

On-page/On-site SEO SEO Content Writing Code Optimizing Inbound Links operational needs.

This is also sometimes known as on-site SEO. This essentially consists of techniques related to the improvement of the layout of the homepage through maintenance, repair and overhaul (MRO) features in your comprehensive and other important pages of the website. The central concerns that are dealt with in on-page SEO or on-site SEO include headings, subheadings, page titles, content display, organization of the written content, and internal link configuration. This process also includes the usage of keywords, ERP solution, you can avoid costly unscheduled downtime. First, automatically gather usage data and track where the tool or equipment is used throughout your shop floor. The goal of on-page SEO is to improve the on-site elements that are important for ranking, as those are taken into account by search engines Then, based on automatic alerts that remind you of upcoming and pending maintenance, when they index and rank websites that are to be displayed in the search engine result pages generate work orders and schedule labor and materials for planned maintenance when you have the parts and bandwidth to take the machine offline. With additional features, such as repair documentation linked to the work order and maintenance cost tracking and visibility. Our ERP solution can help you maximize equipment utilization.

Content has become the central aspect of SEO, as search engines want to provide only the best results to the search engine users, and they

have come to the conclusion that having amazing and original content is one of the aspects to prove a website's quality. It is, quite literally, the most A need to increase capacity is a good problem for any manufacturer to have. Rather stressed-over factor of the SEO industry nowadays.

than investing in new personnel, machines and floor space to handle the new workload, There are so many myths regarding this rather simple concept of writing natural and relevant content. These myths include a mythical word count, manufacturers should first consider increasing plant capacity to 100% with a comprehensive phantom keyword density and many more. SEO content writing is so often, and so conveniently marred, by unethical practices of immoral ERP and MES solutions. This strategy is a less expensive and more flexible approach for stuffing of keywords to gain higher visibility on search engines that the entire concept of SEO crumbles. So often, the merit of an original, well-written content is tainted by these practices, it has become almost a novelty to find good, well-written content.

Content is the foundation of search engine optimization, as well as of lead generation and email marketing. Content helps you enhance your campaign and use a subtle approach to address your potential customers. Unlike promotional campaigns, content writing is focused on the readers and the possibility of solving a problem by providing relevant information.

There are many different content formats. The choice of type of content to implement in your internet marketing strategy depends on your business needs and on your target audience, as you want to produce content that will generate the best outcome among your target group. Here are some tips to help you in creating quality website content:

Provide attention-grabbing headlines Keep the writing mistakes free

Pay attention to the formatting

Add call-to-action buttons on prominent places on the page. Having great content helps you improve your search engine optimization efforts and appeal to your customers.

This will help you generate quality leads and improve the reputation among the website visitors. Great content should fulfill a need, answer a question, inform and educate. Content writing is also an excellent foundation for social media marketing, which will result in increase in shares, leading to higher traffic volume. Ultimately, your efforts will result in increasing brand awareness on the online market, which is an amazing way to boost your business and dominate search results. 7. Deployment Options to Consider When Your Hardware Needs to be Replaced

CHAPTER FIFTEEN

Code optimization

Code optimization refers to re-setting of your website HTML. The benefits of code optimization lead to a two-fold benefit system. Firstly, the One of the most compelling events that lead to investing in new ERP software is that hardware websites take less long to load. This is often the biggest factor, which affects the performance and the incoming traffic on a website. failure or a notification from your vendor that your hardware is no longer supported. Secondly, code optimization enables search engines to easily understand and comprehend the content given on your website. The higher is typically associated with a business that

runs a legacy ERP system. When your hardware has no understandability and accessibility rate of the content leads to better visibility on search engines. The search engines can easily adapt and apply longer viable, there are several courses of action: the algorithms on the given content, as there is no hindrance caused by useless code cluttering. Inbound links •
Buy replacement hardware and continue running your old software

• Look for a third-party vendor that will repair and support your old hardware Websites thrive on link building and/or link development. This is important part of SEO, as links are considered to be a vote of trust, which means •
Consider updating both your hardware and your ERP software so that a website that has a lot of links pointing to it must have done something to deserve those links. Yet, there are similarities to the dilemma of SEO content writing, torn between quantity and quality. The best link development is based on good When hardware fails or becomes excessively unstable, the mindset of owners and business   quality, informative content. In direct contrast to this is the onslaught of useless, inexpensive links, which offer little or no relevance to the website. Their only purpose is to clutter the website with several links, giving the false impression of authority and

short-lived relevance. managers often consider updating both your hardware and ERP software. To most, Good, relevant content leads to establishing the true authority of your website, which ultimately leads to obtaining a good position on the search. This failure is a sign to upgrade to a modern ERP solution. Engine listings and other websites naturally want to link back to you. Earning natural, non-paid links is the goal of true search engine optimization. An effective SEO will lead to inbound links who have an editorial right to be there.

CHAPTER SIXTEEN

Origin and history of search engine optimization

The basic, underlying concept of SEO, or search engine optimization, began tentatively in the mid-1990s. The very first search engines, after the

webmasters submitted the names and the URLs of their websites, began scanning and indexing the websites with the help of 'spiders', which On premise (in-house) based hardware and software served the purpose of 'crawling' a page. These essentially worked like scanning agents. The spiders skimmed through the content of the website and scanned the links given on the website. All this information was stored and submitted for indexing.• Buying and implementing new software and having it hosted in a data center, Once the spider downloaded the essentials of any given webpage, it was sorted and analyzed on the search engine's own server. This sorting and often with managed services directly from the software vendor analysis was then forwarded to the indexer, which, in turn, extracted and focused on the important details of the content, like word count, keyword dMoving to the Cloud or SaaS platform by renting both the software and hardware from a vendor hosting new software in a data center and using the software vendor's managed services has become a popular alternative to on premise ERP. Hosted services address most of the today, search engines incorporate and use sophisticated, highly sensitive algorithms to identify and screen the best, high quality content and links given on the websites. The early versions of algorithms, though, functioned primarily based on the data provided by webmasters. This information upfront hardware costs associated with a pure on premise deployment, eliminating the included Meta tags, which often led to the inaccurate representation of the actual content of the website. This often led to misconstrued results. Issue of end-of-life hardware, while still allowing for long-term amortization of the software Therefore, in the beginning, search engines system was often breached due to these weaknesses and, therefore, irrelevant links were added to licenses, training, implementation costs and control of updates. the search pages listings as a result. Back then, it was much easier to manipulate the search engines algorithms to obtain higher search engine rankings.

CHAPTER SEVENTEEN

Present-day algorithms: Non-disclosure

Managed services from your software vendor provides for software updates and patches. The constant manipulation, as expected, hit the quality of the search engines. Search engines relied on webmasters to provide truthful Operating system maintenance is also performed by the vendor. The vendor will be an expert representation of their content. However, it only led to a great level of link manipulation. This eventually created the need to develop stricter, more in the software and typically do a better, faster and more frequent job of keeping your refined mathematical algorithms. The search engines strove to eliminate the need to rely on thinly veiled concepts like keyword density, which could be easily manipulated and used against the policies of search engine listings. software up to date. Hosting centers can also provide fully redundant systems, backups, Internet service and power. If necessary, they can also provide physically independent locations that ensure protection from natural disasters, such as earthquakes, tornadoes and hurricanes. The downsides to hosted implementations are: • Continued exposure to strict confidentiality or regulatory concerns

• The cost of hosting over a 15-year period will exceed the cost of on premise hardware

• The hardware costs are not able to be capitalized Search engines now function on extremely complex ranking systems and work along strict rules of keeping the algorithms under wraps. Google, Bing, and Yahoo! are known for not revealing the specifics of their current algorithms. By the year 2004, several search engines adopted a number of undisclosed complex factors to their ranking systems in order to avoid link and rank manipulation and false representation.

Three types of SEO Based on the different approaches and results, there are three different types of SEO. These include: 1. White hat SEO 2. Black hat SEO, 3. Grey hat SEO

White hat SEO

White hat SEO relates to the use of techniques and

approaches, which are within the acceptable bounds of search engine rules and regulation. Newer SaaS and Cloud solutions perhaps get more press than any other deployment option.

White hat SEO, as the name suggests, functions along purely the rightful means and does not over-step the confines of search engine algorithms, guidelines and policies. The upside of a pure Cloud-based solution is the almost complete lack of an IT footprint: The techniques used in white hat SEO include writing high quality, informative and original content. The content is well written, lucid, and no software or database updates, no backup or redundancy concerns and certainly no interest, and it avoids shortcuts like plagiarism. The keywords are used naturally and wherever required. There are no haphazard hardware concerns. SaaS and Cloud solutions are relatively painless to maintain throwing-around of keywords and irregular high keyword density. Other techniques used include HTML code optimization, better structuring of the content and good, quality link building based on content and relevance. However, there are several downsides to Cloud implementations. Cost is a key issue. While White hat SEO leads to a gradual but steady and a permanent standing in the search engine rankings, while strictly following guidelines and Cloud or SaaS solutions do have a much lower initial cost of purchase (all you really have to pay for up front is the training and implementation), roughly a SaaS or Cloud system's total

cost of ownership over a 15-year period will be twice the cost of an on premise solution. Black hat SEO, as the name suggests quite clearly, refers to the use of conflicting techniques, which are quick shortcuts to gaining high search rankings and links. Black hat SEO thrives on misrepresentation and manipulation, as it mainly targets the weaknesses and the loopholes in the The higher vendor costs are offset to some extent by reduced soft costs for updates, algorithms of search engines. These techniques and methods are in unswerving clash with the rules and regulations of free-and-fair search engine optimization maintenance, etc. Finally, keep in mind many vendors require a two to four year subscription The techniques used in black hat SEO include providing spam links, giving the false impression of a highly authoritative and highly relevant commitment. Black hat SEO amasses several useless links in order to build links, while no thought is given to the quality of the links. Other techniques employed in black hat SEO are high keyword density and keyword stuffing. The content quality is severely tampered with, keywords are interjected A few key downsides of Cloud solutions are: throughout the text leading to haphazard, choppy, and meaningless content. • It is often the case that SaaS solutions do not perform as quickly as an on premise solution. For companies that are used to instantaneous key stroke responses, this can be frustrating. It is particularly apparent in heads down back office situationsBlack hat SEO leads to quick but short-lived search engine rankings, and it can be penalized by search engines.

• If your business is short on cash or if you are not happy with the vendor, there are no options to go off-serviceAnother interesting kind of SEO is the grey hat SEO. This occurs where the realms of white hat and black hat SEO overlap and merge.

This type of SEO functions by incorporating techniques, which go undetected by search engine algorithms. However, they profusely

• You do not own your data. If you decide to switch vendors, your data stays in focus on improving search engine listings and rankings only. The focus is not on producing well-written and original content at all. Mistaken belief about SEO the Cloud. You must firmly understand your ability transfer your current Cloud data to the new service provider.

There is often a lot of misunderstanding regarding what

SEO can truly achieve. There are many unanswered questions, ambiguous hopes and, more often than not, unrealistic expectations attached to the results of SEO. There are limitations and gains in SEO and it is important to understand what they really mean and entail. It is necessary to realize that SEO can only achieve what is realistically As a final point, don't forget to understand the IT complexity of the system you are buying. possible. Attributing SEO and its results to unrealistic, magical proportions is often a recurrent problem. Some vendors require the customer to buy, install and support their own ERP database. There is a great level of subjectivity when it comes to SEO. Often webmasters and content developers complain that SEO does not Others embed a database that the end user does not have to maintain. deliver according to what it boasts of. SEO does not claim to be magic and it does not function in the concrete world of direct and equal action and reaction. That being said, it is vital to clear misconceptions about what SEO can truly achieve and what it cannot achieve.

With all this being said, there is no one right solution. On premise is affordable and comes with a sense of total control. Cloud is easy, but comes with a higher price and some control SEO can and will most assuredly lead to better user experience. It will increase the user friendliness of your website. However, it will not and there are security concerns. More and more, we are seeing manufacturers lean toward a hybrid to make your website completely and undeniably irresistible to search engines, so you cannot pin unrealistic hopes of high ranks immediately. SEO thrives on good and extensive research. If you have spent a considerable amount of time researching and highlighting the best option: purchase the software licenses outright and own your data, but host software in a data center with managed services from the software vendor.

It is difficult to predict your company's future hardware needs, so when it comes time naturally throughout the content body of your website, SEO will improve the rankings of your website slowly and steadily over the period of a few to evaluate new ERP vendors, find one that offers all three options: on premise, hosted months, even a year. However, this will not lead to the immediate soaring of your website to the highest ranks within a few weeks. SEO will not be services or SaaS/Cloud. A software vendor that offers all three deployment options will lead to a sudden and drastic improvement. offer you flexibility and scalability.

SEO functions on extensive planning and it is a costly

process.

Do not be under the impression that SEO will be an inexpensive process, which will incorporate the use of regular, free directory submissions. Even though SEO is not part of paid advertising, it still requires assets to be invested in the realization of SEO strategy. You might need to hire experts or assistance to help you with content writing or code optimization, which will require payment. However, even if you implement SEO strategy on your own, you will need time to spend in performing different SEO tasks, which can again be costly.

There is no secret 'keyword density' that will alleviate all your problems and suddenly make your content visible in all search engines. There is no secret 'word count' that the search engines love and fall for every time.

All content structuring, keyword density and word count varies from one subject to the next. The only goal is to make the content sound interesting, readable, and understandable. The goal is to make the content likable by readers while also optimizing it for search engine robots. There is more to SEO than just keyword density, word count, and inbound links.

CHAPTER EIGHTEEN

Conclusion

With all this being said if taken into thorough consideration, will have a great impact in your online marketing. However, Effective SEO, in today's world, is literally impossible without the inclusion of social media channels and link building with off-site channels. These off-site channels include social platforms like Facebook, Twitter, Instagram, LinkedIn, or content sharing platforms, such as Reddit, ScoopIt.

ABOUT THE AUTHOR

Odunaya Adesesan

I moved from handling my businesses from physical marketing to owning a wonderful online marketing place that earns me thousands of dollars monthly. The question is how did I go about this. I became more successful in my online marketing after implementing the keys and strategies that's listed in this book. You too can do better by also growing your business online.

www.ingramcontent.com/pod-product-compliance
Lightning Source LLC
Chambersburg PA
CBHW072143170526
45158CB00004BA/1483